CW00373601

YOUTH SEF
MANAGEMᴇɴ ɪ

Aspects of structure, organisation, and development

THE REPORT OF THE BRUNEL
MANAGEMENT AND DEVELOPMENT PROJECT

YOUTH SERVICE
MANAGEMENT

Aspects of structure, organisation, and development

THE REPORT OF THE BRUNEL
MANAGEMENT AND DEVELOPMENT PROJECT

Simon Bradford
and
Michael Day

YOUTH · WORK · PRESS

Cover design by Sanjay Kukadia

Printed and published by Youth Work Press
17–23 Albion Street, Leicester LE1 6GD
Telephone 0533.471200

© 1991
ISBN 0 86155 139 7
£5.95

YOUTH • WORK • PRESS *is a publishing imprint of the National Youth Agency*

Contents

Tables and illustrations

Acknowledgments

THE authors wish to thank: the chief education officers, heads of youth services, and members of staff of the six participating authorities; the joint sponsors of the Management and Development Project—the Department of Education and Science and the Welsh Office; the chairs and members of the Steering Group; Professor Elliott Jaques, Project Consultant; and Martin Hening HMI, Assessor.

We are grateful to colleagues in the Brunel Institute of Organisation and Social Studies for their encouragement and intellectual stimulus during the time this work was being undertaken. We are especially grateful to Margaret Hatswell, Project Secretary, who served in the front line in dealing with the many telephone calls and visitors.

The Project Steering Group

Chairs

Walter Miller (until October 1985)
Dilys Wood (October 1985 to January 1987)
Michael Malt (from January 1987)
Department of Education and Science

Members

Pat Barry
Head of Youth Service, Ealing

Simon Bradford
Research Fellow and Project Officer

Michael Day
Director, Brunel Training Consultative Unit, and Project Supervisor

Martin Hening, HMI
Assessor

Geoffrey Hepworth
Chairman, Brunel Training Consultative Unit, and County Youth and Community Adviser, Surrey

Geoffrey Jones
Adviser for Youth Education, West Glamorgan

John Roberts
Senior Community Education Officer, Walsall

David Smith
National Council for Voluntary Youth Services

Gillian Stamp
Director, Brunel Institute of Organisation and Social Studies

The participating authorities

London boroughs: Croydon, Waltham Forest
Metropolitan borough: Walsall
Counties: Surrey, Warwickshire, West Glamorgan

1

Background

THE Management and Development Project, funded by the Department of Education and Science and the Welsh Office, was located in the Brunel Training Consultative Unit (BTCU), part of the Brunel Institute of Organisation and Social Studies (BIOSS). The three-year project, which commenced in April 1985, was established after extensive consultation with the principal officers of the authorities sponsoring the unit, with Professor Elliott Jaques, Director of BIOSS, and with BTCU staff. They were invited to consider how the management training needs of the youth service's most senior staff might inform the development of a training programme for those staff. These early consultations suggested that any worthwhile development of the service, and any thorough understanding of its work, its organisation, its management, and its role relationships, must involve a recognition that:

- High levels of management expertise are required at both officer and youth worker levels.
- The service has a large number of part-time staff, paid and voluntary—no other local authority service has so many part-time workers. Such an establishment demands appropriate support and back-up.

- Much management training is divorced from the reality of the day-to-day working situation of youth and community personnel. It is totally inappropriate to construct a training programme in a vacuum.
- The first stage in any management programme would be the articulation and clarification of existing policy in local authority youth services. It was anticipated that the policy of some authorities might be fully articulated while in others it would be more implicit and would need clarification.
- Management structures should arise from the work implied by the execution of these policies. No programme of research could avoid close examination of the present roles of staff in the youth service. Such a scrutiny would need to take account of existing and available resources.
- Management structures could not be viewed as static. They should be considered in relation to potential developments envisaged in the youth service.

These discussions led to the formulation of the research proposals submitted to the DES, which were subsequently reinforced by the findings and recommendations of the Thompson Report.[1] There was clearly a need for a research project examining youth service management, policy, and existing internal role relationships. But the youth service does not operate independently of other services—its work intermeshes with that of other agencies and organisations in the broad field of social education and social welfare. It was recognised that these links and relationships would need to be considered. Questions of how the service monitors its work, and how it provides support structures for its staff in both the full-time and part-time sectors, were likewise taken within the scope of the project so that the nature of existing practice could be determined. It was felt important to seek ways of improving management effectiveness at all levels, in order to enhance service delivery. Finally, the findings of the research should be

[1] *Experience and Participation: report of the Review Group on the Youth Service in England*, London, HMSO, 1982.

made available to as wide a range of local authority youth services as possible, through conferences and publications.

The submission to the DES was backed by the Standing Committee of Sponsors of the Brunel Training Consultative Unit, and, in order to secure the fullest support at chief education officer level, preliminary discussions took place with a number of interested local authorities. The project aimed to collaborate with five local authority youth services in a detailed examination of their operation, from the work of senior management through to the interface between the service and its clients.

The research project was confirmed by the DES in December 1984. A planning group meeting in January 1985 decided that the authorities involved should ideally extend beyond the London and Home Counties region, since this would assist in the consideration of national implications. It was further agreed that at least one authority would be chosen from each of three categories: (1) London boroughs; (2) shire counties; (3) other boroughs.

In consultation with the funding agencies and in discussions with authorities, agreement was reached in principle for the following local authorities to be involved in the project:

Category 1 Croydon and Waltham Forest
Category 2 Surrey, Warwickshire, and West Glamorgan
Category 3 Walsall

Authorities were selected to provide a diverse range of youth services in terms of organisation, size, staffing structure, and provision. While it would not be possible to extrapolate into the total range of provision in England and Wales, it was hoped that the project's findings would apply to the majority of youth services.

A steering group was established to advise and guide the research team, and Professor Elliott Jaques served as consultant.

Initially, the project was funded for two years commencing in April 1985, but a further year's funding was later secured to enable the following research strategy to be adopted.

Years one and two

Phase one. To articulate policies, roles and role relationships, and day-to-day practices of the services concerned; to evaluate service delivery; and to determine statements of principle and generalisations arising from the research (16 months). Consideration would be given to resource allocation and to inter-agency co-operation, especially between the youth service and schools, further education, and other local government agencies.

Phase two. Dissemination strategy: sharing findings with authorities taking part; formulation of development strategies for improving management effectiveness and for providing alternative policies and practice; relating findings to wider issues in management (8 months).

Year three

Phase three. Whereas the second phase was primarily concerned with the promotion of development strategies in the context of the issues raised by the research, the third would be concerned with the step-by-step implementation of change in each of the participating authorities. Throughout this phase, there would be a continuous process of testing and dissemination.

Phase four. The testing of generalisations, concepts, and formulations would necessarily involve a wider range of youth service organisations in England and Wales. A series of conferences and seminars would be arranged, focusing especially on those issues thought to have relevance beyond the authorities involved in the project.

2

Methods and approaches

THE main research method used in the Management and Development Project was *social analysis*, defined by Rowbottom as: 'an activity devoted to gaining scientific understanding of, and thereby facilitating enacted change in social institutions through collaborative exploration by those actors immediately concerned in their working, and an independent analyst'.[1] The social analytic method was developed by Jaques, and is used extensively in the Brunel Institute of Organisation and Social Studies.[2] It provides the opportunity for collaborative exploration of issues identified as problems in a particular social institution. Within a general climate of collaboration, social analysis helps members of an organisation to identify and define the nature and extent of the problems experienced in that organisation. Necessarily, such an approach generates an action framework for bringing about enactable changes in the social institution. These changes may be broadly concerned with: (1) the structure and composition of the organisation; (2) the organisation's aims and functions; (3) authority vested in positions in the organisation; (4) accountability systems and

[1] Ralph Rowbottom, *Social Analysis*, London, Heinemann, 1977, p. 21.
[2] See E. Jaques and W. Brown, *Glacier Project Papers*, London, Heinemann Educational, 1965.

relationships in the organisation; (5) rewards and perquisites given to organisation members; (6) rules and procedures governing the organisation and its work.

The focus of the Brunel project was on policy, organisational structures, roles and role relationships, and the nature of provision for the defined clients of the participating services. In most cases the client group was young people.

Analysis of roles and role relationships

Social analysis was used principally to examine and define roles and role relationships, including individuals' perceptions of how they related to others in the existing structure. Work roles do not exist as separate entities; they are always part of a wider social network and are component parts of role relationships. These relationships are integral to the definition of each role, and they set the boundaries and directions for individual work.

The project sought to explore existing role relationships in participating services with a view to increasing the effectiveness of those services through clarification of perceptions and, where necessary, through change. It was recognised that perceptions and descriptions of role relationships were likely to differ among individuals with the same job title, depending on the context. They were also likely to differ from official definitions. The organisational chart of a particular department or service defines a network of role relationships. Experience shows that these charts cannot be taken at face value because they are often inaccurate, unclear, or outdated.

In the social analytic approach, official statements of role relationships such as those in organisational charts make up the *manifest* social structure. Individual and collective descriptions of perceived role relationships may be termed the *assumed* social structure of the organisation. Social analysis seeks to assist those concerned in clarifying and comparing different perceptions of the role relationships in the organisation. This necessitates the development of a language adequate for the translation of these descriptions into named role relationships (for example, managerial role or co-ordinating role), and one which can, at the same time, allow us to begin to conceptualise what is termed the *extant* social structure. To formulate the extant structure is to move towards a much more precise conception of the roles and role relationships being considered—in one sense, developing a picture of what is really going on in the organisation. Beyond this, and importantly, is the formulation of the *requisite* social structure, whereby roles and role relationships are defined as what they ought to be for the work of the organisation to be undertaken more effectively.

Social analytic procedure

In each participant authority, the approval of the chief education officer was sought for the authority's involvement. Acceptance of the invitation to become involved was communicated by the authority to the project through a memorandum of agreement. Then, after consultation with each youth service staff team, a local project management group (LPMG) was established to advise on and monitor the research, and eventually to consider priorities for the management of change. LPMGs were made up of individuals from different levels of each service, including youth officers and full- and part-time youth workers.

Ground rules consistent with the social analytic method were established. The following statements guided procedure:

- *Agreement to participate as a client will be signified following a meeting between the chief education officer, the principal youth officer and a Brunel representative and will be confirmed in the form of a memorandum of agreement between the project and the chief education officer.*

- *Each local authority youth service department will be invited, following a full staff meeting, to establish a project monitoring group containing* • *a minimum of five individuals representative of all levels and types of*

*work within the service. This will be established and become the local
project management group (LPMG).*

- *There will be no compulsion for any individual to participate in the
  project. Researchers will be invited to undertake the necessary interviews
  in accordance with agreed procedures established by the LPMG.
  Interviews will initially be confidential and any written material will
  require clearing by the individual directly involved before its contents
  are made known to the LPMG. It will be for the LPMG to clear
  material for wider dissemination within the project.*

- *It is assumed that participating youth services, through the chief
  education officer, will establish a procedure in conjunction with the
  LPMG to give due consideration to the findings arising from their
  collaboration in the research.*

- *Any changes endorsed by the youth service concerned will require
  careful implementation and monitoring, and the research staff are
  committed to a programme of assistance in consultancy and support in
  later phases of the project.*

A stage-by-stage procedural sequence for the implementation of the
project, from the initial contact with the authority through to the
consideration of the project's findings, was laid down. The approach
taken is shown in Appendix 1.

Each LPMG advised the researcher and liaised with individuals in
their authority in order to reach agreement on who should be involved
in intensive interviews.

A detailed report of each interview was prepared, and a final version
negotiated with the interviewee. Such negotiation involved cross-
checking with the interviewee to arrive at an accurate account of his or
her work situation. It was the intention to clear these reports for
submission to the LPMG, but it became evident that some interviewees
were very anxious about having their frank spoken submissions recorded
on paper. Many were unwilling, and understandably so, for this material
to go into a more public domain. In only one of the six participating
authorities were individual interviewees prepared to have their views

8   *Youth service management*

conveyed to the LPMG. Revising the interview reports to make them suitable for dissemination would have led to loss of data and devalued their content. For this reason it was decided to collate the various interviews undertaken in each authority to produce a composite report which would contain all the essential material while protecting the anonymity of individuals, though this was clearly more difficult in the case of specialist or single roles such as that of head of service. The composite report provided an overview of many of the management issues associated with roles and role relationships in the services concerned, and one of the bases on which LPMGs would identify any action and change necessary. The local group would then determine whether documentation from the research should be cleared for wider dissemination.

Both the individual interviewees and the LPMG were thus empowered to veto the publication of research documentation at any stage. Overall, this approach generated a sense of ownership, and implied that the participating youth workers and officers were active partners in the project and not merely its research subjects.

Evaluation of service delivery

A second feature of the research design for the project involved 'evaluating the nature of service delivery to young people and other defined clients, as identified in the policy'. Youth service policy, management structure, and provision were seen as the vehicles through which a service is delivered to young people and, in certain cases, to other defined clients. The interface between the service and its clients represented an important focus of the research.

In the second year, finance permitted the project to employ three third-year full-time BSc (Hons) social science undergraduates from Brunel as research assistants during their annual 20-week block of work experience. Each was required to undertake placements in two of the six authorities. In each three-week placement they would be involved in three different kinds of youth work situation determined by the LPMG.

The research assistants were required to examine youth work practice, and their role in each location comprised six broad elements:

- participant observation of what the staff did in relation to the club, centre, or project, and their relationships with young people or other defined clients;
- appraisal of the extent of involvement, participation, and social education being offered, the nature of the curriculum, the programme of activities, and so on;
- shadowing the full-time worker in relation to his or her duties;
- preparation of statistics and information concerning provision usage, financial arrangements, opening times;
- undertaking interviews with three part-time staff members and group interviews with young people about the nature of the work observed;
- at authority and provision level, examining the nature of inter-agency co-operation—that is, between the youth service and other authority services, voluntary organisations, and government agencies such as MSC.

Arrangements for the placements were made by each LPMG, and the three situations in each authority were chosen to reflect different types of work undertaken, such as a club, centre, or project. The latter might, for example, involve detached work, a counselling agency, an unemployment scheme, or a drama workshop. The situations being explored were normally under the direction of a full-time staff member who would be the individual to be shadowed by the research assistants.

Essentially, the placement work required two types of research skill: participant observation and interviewing with individuals and groups.

Participant observation is a powerful research tool for generating ethnographic descriptions and providing insights into the texture and meaning of social situations.[3] The research assistants were well placed

[3] For a full discussion of participant observation, see B. H. Junker, *Fieldwork: an introduction to the social sciences*, Chicago, University of Chicago Press, 1960, or M. Hammersley and P. Atkinson, *Ethnography: principles in practice*, London, Tavistock, 1983.

to work in this way, to approach the young people in the research sites without there being a wide age difference, and to operate effectively with the full- and part-time staff. Shadowing was intended to serve as a vehicle through which the research assistants gained insights into the nature of the work undertaken by youth workers in the course of their duties. This involved the research assistants working in youth centres, in community projects, in a town centre where youth workers undertook detached work, in school youth wings, and in sports projects.

Interviews with part-time staff provided additional illumination of the observations undertaken within the working situations, and the research was further extended by group discussion with young people. All reports prepared as a result of these placements would be presented to the LPMG, and interview material would need to be cleared with the individuals concerned in accordance with the method of social analysis.

From research to consultancy

The composite reports referred to earlier, together with the placement reports provided by the research assistants, became the material used by the LPMGs to examine the management issues arising from the project fieldwork. Once this information was obtained, the role of the research workers changed to that of consultants. In this role, the researchers helped LPMGs to examine the service implications of the issues identified and to determine appropriate courses of action in any management of change. This approach preserved the role of the LPMG as the client, with the researcher assisting in the dissemination of the material and presentation to various groups within each local authority. Feedback was provided to full-time staff at authority meetings, to the groups involved in the fieldwork, to management committees, and in some instances to councillors.

3

Elements of theory

YOUTH services are hierarchical organisations with a number of managerial levels. The project took as its theoretical starting point a definition of *bureaucracy* proposed by Jaques: 'a hierarchically stratified managerial employment system in which people are employed to work for a wage or salary: that is to say a stratified employment hierarchy with at least one manager who in turn has a staff of employed subordinates'.[1] There is considerable evidence from research undertaken at Brunel that in bureaucratic organisations the responsibilities of individuals and their relationships with others are frequently ill-defined and ambiguous.[2] Often this is interpreted as flexibility and is seen as a good thing. Personal relationships in an organisation or a unit may be such that people get along well and the work itself is completed. However, the loose definition of roles, relationships, and responsibilities leaves the organisation extremely vulnerable to staff changes, and it is very difficult to distinguish between personality problems and organisational

---

[1] Elliott Jaques, *A General Theory of Bureaucracy*, London, Heinemann, 1976, p. 49.
[2] See, for example, D. Billis, G. Bromley, A. Hey, and R. Rowbottom, *Organising Social Services Departments*, London, Heinemann, 1980; and D. Billis, *Welfare Bureaucracies*, London, Heinemann, 1984.

problems in these circumstances. In these respects, youth services are typical bureaucracies.

A general conclusion from the Management and Development Project is that many organisational problems in youth services can be traced to inadequate specification of responsibilities, and a correspondingly inadequate appreciation by individuals of their own and others' work responsibilities. This leads to situations characterised by high levels of uncertainty for individuals. Although job descriptions are used, actual responsibilities are often left to individuals to find by trial and error. The youth service should, of course, be capable of a flexible response to client need, and staff should have sufficient space for the development of creative work. But there is a danger of flexibility becoming an 'anything goes' approach, with little attention being paid to the proper marking out of work boundaries. It is always necessary to balance creative space with structure and boundaries. This task is fundamental to managerial work.

Work: prescribed and discretionary elements

Any usable definition or understanding of work in organisations must take into account the choices to be made by individuals undertaking the work and the organisational constraints within which they undertake it. The following definition of work is useful: 'The exercise of discretion within prescribed limits in order to achieve a goal within a maximum target completion time.'[3] This formula accommodates the individual and organisational elements of work, and points to the *prescribed* and *discretionary* elements which underlie any work in organisations. *Discretion* refers to the necessary choices and judgments that individuals must make when working. The *prescribed limits* are the boundaries which are set around work: policies, rules, procedures, methods, and so on. They provide a shape or form to a piece of work by confirming what is required of the individual worker. As such, they reduce uncertainty

[3] Quoted in G. Stamp, 'Some observations on the career path of women', *Journal of Applied Behavioral Science*, vol. 22, no. 4 (1986), 385–396.

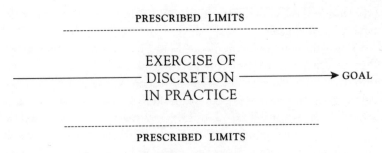

EXERCISE OF
DISCRETION ⟶ GOAL
IN PRACTICE

PRESCRIBED LIMITS

Figure 1. *Discretion within prescribed limits*

and mark out a definite field in which people are expected to act. Thus, prescribed limits free individuals to exercise discretion and to make choices in order to complete their work. This can be depicted as in Figure 1. In practice, and in the youth service, these elements are often unclear:

> *Nobody's ever said anything about how the work here should be done … They leave it up to me and they tell me if I get it wrong …*
>
> Centre-based worker

> *I think the work of the centre is OK because nobody, the management committee or the youth officer, hasn't said anything … But they haven't said what sort of thing they expect anyway. I think it must be OK.*
>
> Centre-based worker

Limits left undeclared, and discovered or acknowledged only when breached, are common in youth services. Such a situation reflects a failure to provide an adequate or appropriate support structure for workers.

Levels of work and organisational structure

A common-sense view of organisations would probably identify different types of work expected of members at different levels. A typical public-service organisation like the youth service might be seen as in Figure 2.

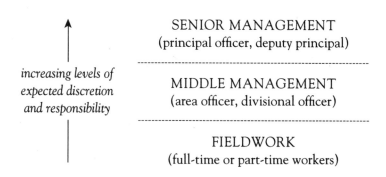

Figure 2. *A common-sense hierarchy of work levels*

This simple diagram suggests, rightly, that the work of senior managers is different from that of middle managers, which in turn is different from that of fieldworkers, and that these different types of work carry different levels of discretion and responsibility. But it does not help in defining the functions of such discretion and responsibility, or precisely what might be expected of people doing the work.

Work levels or work strata theory developed at Brunel provided important insights for the project, helping not only to clarify the kinds of work appropriate to different levels of youth service organisations, but also to identify the kinds of decision about work that individuals are required to make.[4] The theory describes a number of qualitatively different levels or types of work in organisations, which provide a basis for distinguishing responsibilities at different points of an organisation. The levels are hierarchically arranged, and it is argued that this hierarchy of work levels exists naturally in organisations. The levels are discontinuous; that is to say, a move from one level to the next demands a conceptually different approach to work by the individual concerned. A move from lower to higher work levels involves a broadening of the objectives to be met and the factors to be taken into account by the worker. Figure 3 shows the work levels and briefly defines the kind of work expected at each level. Each level (except level 1) provides the

[4] For a more detailed treatment of work levels, see Jaques, *A General Theory of Bureaucracy*.

WORK LEVEL	TYPE OF WORK EXPECTED
5: Comprehensive field coverage	Making comprehensive provision of services in a general field of need in a society, such as housing, education, leisure.
4: Comprehensive service provision	Making comprehensive provision of services of a given kind, according to the need for them, in a geographical area or an organisation.
3: Systematic service provision	Making systematic provision of services of given kinds in a specific location, according to the needs of a flow of actual cases or situations.
2: Situational response	Undertaking work where goals are identified in the light of assessment of the real underlying need in actual situations or circumstances presented.
1: Prescribed output	Undertaking work where goals are specified beforehand or are part of routine requirements.

Figure 3. *Levels of work*

framework or context for the work level below: for example, the level-3 manager provides the context (policy, goals, methods, and so on) in which the level-2 worker operates.

The *highest expected work* and the *basic expected work* (that is, the minimum acceptable work) will determine how many levels of work there need to be in any organisation.

The highest impact that a local authority youth service is expected to make is probably at level 4, although in many youth services it will be at level 3. This will depend on the type and range of service required in any given circumstances. Correspondingly, the basic expected work of youth services seems to vary as well. Generally, one might expect them to be providing a level-2 impact at direct-output or client level—that is to say, a basic professional service. The project showed that in some authorities level-1 work seemed to be expected; in others the important distinction between level-1 and level-2 work had not been recognised, and consequently the expected work level of staff was not always clear.

Work levels and youth service work

Even the most superficial examination of youth service work reveals that there are qualitatively different types of work going on. The main distinctions appear to be between the work of part-time staff, full-time youth workers, area officers, and principal officers. But these distinctions are further complicated by a number of other appointment levels or apparently different types of work, including various grades of part-time staff, senior workers, area workers, team leaders, district officers, deputy officers, and assistant officers. The proliferation of these roles has made youth service structures extremely complex in some local authorities. Work levels theory provides a basis for clarifying the work of such roles, and locating them requisitely in youth service structures.

Some caveats are necessary here. First, the level of work expected of an individual—the work for which that individual is *accountable*—may not correspond with his or her capability. People may well be over- or under-employed in their organisation, and many examples of mismatch are evident in youth services.

Second, we need to differentiate between *grading level* and *level of work*. Grading is concerned with levels of pay or remuneration rather than work levels as described here. It is common, however, for the grading system to be regarded as the same thing as the organisational structure. In reality, levels of work required in an organisation rather than grades should determine its structure. Different grades are probably necessary within the same work level.

Appendix 2 applies work levels theory to typical youth service roles. This table may not reflect the wide variations in the work expected of roles in different services, and it should therefore be adapted to specific circumstances. It should be looked at in conjunction with the following brief consideration of work levels as they relate to the youth service.

Level 4: comprehensive service provision

We suggest that this is the highest expected work of youth services. This does not mean that there are no heads of service with a capability extending beyond level 4. The point is that they are likely to be accountable for delivering a level-4 service. At this level, a head of service might be expected to ask and respond to this question: 'What kind of youth service is required in this authority in the light of existing and potential need?' Level-4 heads will be expected to compare existing provision with new ways of providing a more effective service. This probably means work concerned with service development throughout an authority, and accountability for service policies; identifying service priorities and developments; budgeting and costing development work; planning, implementing, and evaluating developments; controlling the staff establishment; restructuring where necessary; and directly managing level-3 workers.

Level 3: systematic service provision

Level-3 roles are often the most difficult to occupy. As one youth officer interviewed during the project put it, 'I feel like the meat in the sandwich.' The level-3 officer bridges the gap between the policy-makers and the field. He or she will be concerned with managing the tension between the requirements of higher-level policy and the needs of client groups, and will often feel pulled in both directions. Level-3 work is one step removed from direct or continuous client contact. It is essentially concerned with ideas about the needs of client groups rather than with hands-on response to those needs. It is primarily oriented to establishing systems, contexts, and frameworks within which direct work with young people can be done effectively by workers operating at levels 1 and 2. It is to do with making the most of given resources and people in order to realise the higher-level policies— emanating from level 4—which define the kind of youth service required. This means that level-3 staff will probably be involved in directly managing staff at level 2 and in exercising some control over resources and plant.

Work at this level includes accountability for developing an integrated area or unit mission in accordance with service policy; working closely with level-4 managers on development matters; furthering level-4 policies through the area or unit; involvement in the appointment of area or unit staff; staff development throughout the area or unit; and planning, managing, and reviewing the area or unit budget and expenditure.

Level 2: situational response

This is what might be regarded as basic professional work: work concerned with appraising individual situations or cases (young people, centres, clubs, groups, staff members) as they are encountered, and judging the appropriate response. In this it differs from level-3 work, which is concerned with sequences or flows of situations rather than discrete cases.

Work at this level means accountability for judging and assessing the needs of individuals or groups; working out appropriate responses to individuals or groups within given policy; involvement in level-1 appointments; staff development at level 1; and managing level-1 staff.

The view taken during the project was that all professionally qualified youth workers, both full- and part-time, should be working at level 2. And it is clear from the project's work that some part-time staff are expected to operate at this level, undertaking work similar to that of their full-time colleagues. This raises important questions about selection, staff development, remuneration, and training. If part-time staff are *expected* to perform level-2 work, their *ability* to do so must be properly recognised: they must be enabled to develop the requisite skills and expertise, and should be provided with proper support.

Level 1: prescribed output

Essentially, level-1 work involves undertaking particular and specified programmes of activity, the outcome of which can be largely identified beforehand. At this level the individual will be accountable for the performance of specific tasks prescribed by a level-2 manager or routinely expected of them as part of their job. Such work may be skilled and may require individuals to have specific knowledge and attitudes.

Work on the Management and Development Project suggests that some service managers, units, and full-time staff expect no more than level-1 work from part-time staff and volunteers. In other situations, however, the expectation seems to be that part-time staff, particularly those in charge of a club or unit, should be able and willing to undertake work at level 2. Undoubtedly there is a need for level-1 work to be done. But youth services should be clearer and more explicit about the level at which part-time staff are expected to operate. This is particularly important given that part-time staff are at the primary point of delivery of the service itself. Selection, induction, training, and support programmes must be designed to match the expected work level of these staff.

Matching work and managerial levels

As well as clarifying the kind of work expected or required in particular jobs, work levels theory can make a contribution to questions about managerial levels in the youth service.

There is a need to be specific about the nature of *managerial roles*. This is frequently unclear in the youth service, despite the fact that many roles are described as managerial. A particular model of a line managerial role was adopted in the project, one sufficiently specific for clarifying the nature of managerial relationships in the youth service. According to this model, a main-line managerial relationship involves the line manager in:

- assigning duties and responsibilities to managees—'building' the managee's job;
- appraising the managee's performance and abilities—judging how he or she is doing;
- forwarding staff development of managees—helping them 'grow in the job';

and it implies authority to:

- take part in the selection of managees, including recruitment and interviewing;

- prescribe managees' work in as much detail as necessary—'shape' the managee's job;
- initiate the managee's promotion, transfer, or dismissal.

Work levels theory suggests that line manager and managee should always belong to different but adjoining levels. If they are located in the same work level, it quickly becomes difficult for the so-called manager to act appropriately. He or she is unable to take the overview of the managee's work which would be permitted by being located in the next-higher work level. In effect the so-called line manager is unable to make managerial decisions, irrespective of personal capability and skills.

Youth services often have too many managerial levels, these sometimes being confused with grading levels such as those advocated by JNC. There is at most a need for only three main-line managerial levels in these organisations. If the highest expected work is at level 4, the organisational structure represented in Figure 4 is likely to be appropriate. Deputy principal officers, district officers, senior workers, and team leaders are probably not requisitely located as main-line managers, although they may be involved in other types of authority relationship—as monitors, co-ordinators, or supervisors, for example (see Appendix 3). The main point here is that these are requisitely off-line roles. Various kinds of authority relationship undoubtedly operate in youth services, sometimes without being clearly specified or

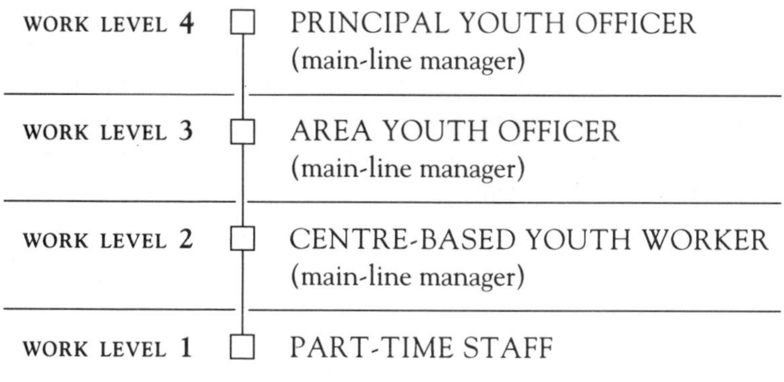

WORK LEVEL 4	☐	PRINCIPAL YOUTH OFFICER (main-line manager)
WORK LEVEL 3	☐	AREA YOUTH OFFICER (main-line manager)
WORK LEVEL 2	☐	CENTRE-BASED YOUTH WORKER (main-line manager)
WORK LEVEL 1	☐	PART-TIME STAFF

Figure 4. *An appropriate organisational structure for youth services*

understood. They are sometimes a source of great tension, and youth service managers should carefully assess the needs of various situations and specify relationships clearly.

Organisational culture and values

Structure is not the only important aspect of an organisation. There is also its culture to take into account: its history, its characteristic values, beliefs, and assumptions, and its ways of doing things.[5] Our work has found that cultures vary considerably from one youth service to another, and between individual units or projects within a service.

The ways in which youth services get their work done and conduct their business depend to a great extent on the systems that they adopt—for example, recruitment and selection practices, or promotion systems. These systems embody and symbolise the service's underlying values, and the experiences of service members and clients will be shaped by the way these systems operate. Questions about these systems are therefore often tied up with questions about values. Does service delivery reflect equal opportunities principles? Do remuneration schemes operate fairly for part-time and full-time staff? Do staff development programmes properly value individuals in the service?

Managerial work in any youth service is both influenced by and is an expression of its culture. Managers are involved in the design and implemenation of the organisation's systems, and it is important that they are clear about the values expressed through these systems. They should also be aware that their own managerial style and approach is an expression of values, whether personal or organisational, and will be interpreted as such by staff.

[5] For a full discussion of organisational cultures, see G. Morgan, *Images of Organisation*, Beverly Hills, Sage, 1987; and C. Handy, *Understanding Organisations*, 2nd edn, Harmondsworth, Penguin, 1982.

4

The fieldwork programme

THE project's main method of data collection was through interviews, either with individuals or with small groups. These provided an opportunity for collaborative exploration of concerns and issues.

At the outset, the project's research staff felt it important to undertake in-depth interviews with each of the six heads of service, and this work was completed before they embarked on the programme of interviews with other staff. Through these interviews the researchers were able to map out each service in terms of its roles, structure, and organisational relationships, the nature of its provision, and its relationships with other sections, departments, and agencies. They were also able to check out their own perceptions of each service as gained from organisational charts, policy documents, and the like. These interviews also gave heads of service the opportunity to raise their own concerns about their services and to identify what they perceived to be difficulties or problems.

Individual and group interviews with other staff were intended to provide as detailed a picture as possible of the following areas:

- role dimensions and boundaries;
- authority and accountability;

- work expected of individuals;
- tasks and duties;
- relationships with managers and managees and others;
- problems and difficulties.

It was anticipated that extensive interviewing would allow a composite picture of organisational life in each of the six youth services to be built up. This would serve to identify and clarify problems which could subsequently be worked on by LPMGs and more widely in the authorities concerned. This later work would contribute to the development of models of requisite youth service organisation, with a view to implementation in the participant services.

Interview programmes were arranged by LPMGs. Interviewees were selected to provide as broad a sweep of each service as possible, covering all levels of the organisation and taking account of the number of roles at each level. Interviewees were approached individually on behalf of the LPMG and invited to take part in the programme.

The majority of interviews were with individuals. However, group interviews were undertaken with part-time workers because of the large numbers of these staff in each authority. Several groups of management committee members were also interviewed. Tables 1 and 2 give the numbers and distribution of interviews undertaken in each authority.

Table 1. *Interview numbers**

AUTHORITY	TOTAL	INDIVIDUAL	GROUP
Croydon	20	16	4
Surrey	18	12	6
Walsall	26	19	7
Waltham Forest	21	18	3
Warwickshire	17	16	1
West Glamorgan	22	19	3

* In several cases repeat interviews were undertaken with individuals in order to clarify or extend particular issues.

Table 2. *Distribution of interviews by role of interviewee*

AUTHORITY	a	b	c	d	e
Croydon	6	4	5	3	2
Surrey	1	3	6	7	1
Walsall	0	16	5	5	0
Waltham Forest	0	3	12	4	2
Warwickshire	0	1	8	6	2
West Glamorgan	0	8	10	4	0

Key: (a) management committee members; (b) voluntary and part-time youth workers; (c) full-time qualified youth workers; (d) youth officers, including head of service; (e) senior education department staff.

It should be noted in passing that, when the interview programme was undertaken, very few senior and middle management posts in the six youth services were occupied by women, black people, or people with disabilities. Given the youth service's current espousal of equal opportunities principles, it is clear that this might represent a contradiction.[1]

Each interview was written up in detail by the project research staff, in accordance with the procedure described in Chapter 2. The report was subsequently sent to the interviewee, who was asked to check that it gave an accurate account of how he or she saw the issues which had been identified and discussed. In the case of group interviews, the report was made available to the group for discussion and comment. At this point, interviewees were invited to make any necessary amendments or modifications to the text. This process of refinement was continued until an agreed version was reached.

Throughout the programmes, the confidentiality of interviews was emphasised to interviewees. This facilitated the discussion of some

[1] This is confirmed by recent BTCU research undertaken for the Commission for Racial Equality. This work will be published in a forthcoming book by M. L. Day, S. J. Bradford, and L. Eaton, *Embroidered in Gold: equal opportunities and the youth service*.

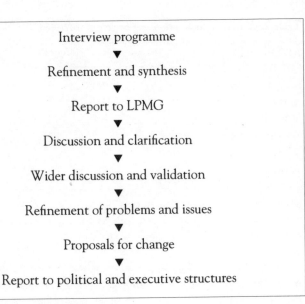

Interview programme
▼
Refinement and synthesis
▼
Report to LPMG
▼
Discussion and clarification
▼
Wider discussion and validation
▼
Refinement of problems and issues
▼
Proposals for change
▼
Report to political and executive structures

Figure 5. *The processing of research data*

highly sensitive issues. Ironically, this very sensitivity inhibited the dissemination of much of the material derived from the interview programme. In five of the six authorities, it was necessary to write up a synthesis of the issues identified, in the form of a covering report for presentation to the LPMGs.

A large quantity of written material was generated by the fieldwork. All of it was shared with LPMGs, which took on the function of marshalling and managing this material. It provided the basis for discussion and for wide consultation with staff in the participating authorities, and helped to identify the direction for further exploration of substantive themes arising from the research. Figure 5 shows the processes by which this research data was transformed into practical proposals for change.

5

Key issues in youth service organisation

*F*IELDWORK in the six participating authorities revealed a number of frequently recurring themes and problems in the organisation and delivery of the youth service. Poor working relationships, cynicism towards managers or managees, high staff turnover, a general sense of low morale, and feelings of 'not knowing where we're going' were common in the youth services in which we worked. Many such issues can be traced to more fundamental problems which appear to characterise youth service organisation. This chapter looks at five main themes which emerged from the project's work, the importance of which was confirmed by conference work undertaken during the project.

The definition of work

I have been here for 18 months now. Nobody has ever checked on me to see how I am doing. I think I am doing what is expected but I couldn't be sure.

Youth and community worker

I like the fact that nobody bothers me—you know, I can just get on with it. But at the same time you just don't know how you are doing or even if you are doing what you are supposed to do.

Youth worker

I look at all the stuff that comes into me and how much of it is import-ant I don't know. It's a question of moving from one thing to another really. Crisis management I suppose.

Youth and community officer

Discussions at various levels in the youth service indicate that there is a basic lack of clarity concerning the work that is to be done. What is expected of fieldworkers? What is the essential work of youth officers, and how does this differ from that of fieldwork staff? How much of an individual's time should be spent in client contact work and how much in planning or managing, and how should these proportions vary according to work level? Equally important are definitions of the expected work of part-time staff, not least because they represent the primary delivery point for the service itself.

While it is clear that many youth service personnel welcome some autonomy and breadth of discretion in planning and delivering their work, they may also simultaneously acknowledge that the lack of a framework giving direction and purpose often creates needless un-certainty. If the work required or expected of people lacks clarity and is inadequately specified, it will not get done other than by chance and it will be difficult to know how best to establish managerial structures and practices to facilitate and develop the capacity of staff in their work. Line managers have particularly important functions in shaping the work of managees. The process involved in this kind of management is fundamental to the effective organisation and delivery of the youth service. It is a process of transforming ideas and concepts—social education, for example—into action.

Summary points

- There is a need for a greater clarity in the definition of work at all youth service levels.
- Work expectations on individuals must be made explicit.

- There needs to be a clear balance between discretion and prescribed limits applying to individual jobs.
- Management structures and practices must support the identification and execution of the work required.

Managerial levels

The problem is getting decisions about things—money, equipment, and so on, but also whether we can do certain bits of work. I have got a team leader and I am supposed to go to him with all these sorts of things. But usually he says he will have to speak to the area officer to get a decision. Officially the team leader is my boss but I don't see it that way. I suppose he is a sort of mini-boss. If you want something doing or you need something it is usually best to see the area officer. I don't really know why we have team leaders.

Centre-based youth and community worker

I am supposed to be responsible to the deputy principal. It all gets confused because the principal comes straight to us with things ... And if I'm honest we tend to go straight to him if there is a problem. The deputy gets stuck in the middle—a bit like a spare part ... Of course he's got his own work to do and I suppose he just gets on with that. It's all a bit of an anomaly.

Area youth and community officer

These two quotations exemplify a situation which seems endemic in large-scale organisations, and which is common in youth services. The problem centres on the location of managerial levels. In both the youth services to which these quotations relate, the organisational chart indicated that the role of the team leader and the role of the deputy principal were 'on-line'. They were both depicted as full line managerial roles, although unable in practice to sustain this managerial work. Discussions of their work and responsibilities with the staff concerned suggested that in both cases the apparent line manager and managee were operating in the same work level, as represented in Figure 6.

Key issues in youth service organisation   **29**

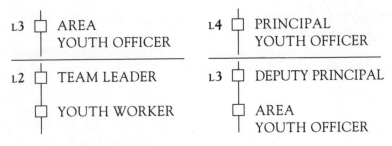

Figure 6. *Inappropriate work levels*

Uncertainty about who one is really accountable to, by-passing, excessively long chains of command, protracted decision-making, a sense of insecurity on the part of those directly involved, role confusion, a feeling of organisational clutter and of stepping on other people's toes are all experiences which result from such doubtful and inappropriate systems of accountability. Indeed, it is unclear whether real accountability exists at all in circumstances like these, all of which were encountered during the project's work.

Conversely, the project identified some situations where there was an absence of a particular managerial level. One important example of this was the absence of level-3 managerial roles in an organisation where the highest expected work is at level 4 and the basic expected work is at level 2. In this case, however, senior practitioners manifestly felt themselves in the position of being expected to undertake some work at level 3. This had some problematic consequences. The senior practitioners felt themselves unable to take an overview of youth workers' work, and did not feel that they had the knowledge of policy and budgetary requirements to fully manage the youth workers. Youth workers, for their part, felt that the senior practitioners were engaged in work substantially similar to their own. They did not recognise senior practitioners as having either the responsibility or the capacity to act as line managers. It was also found that the (notionally) level-4 principal youth officer was often having to double up as service head and middle manager, with an evident stretching of available resources.

The absence of systematic service work at level 3 means that the contextualising and support of fieldwork is not done, or not done adequately. This leads to fieldwork staff operating autonomously. In services where the highest expected work is at level 3, the same contextual and support work is extremely important for level-2 practitioners. Without it, clarity and direction in work is lost.

Summary points

- Managerial roles in youth services should be carefully located and structured.
- Placing managers and managees in the same work level leads to by-passing, role confusion, and tension.
- The absence of a particular level of work in a youth service means that important work may not be undertaken.

Authority relationships

Earlier reference was made to the discrepancies and slippages between organisational structures as depicted in official charts and what might be referred to as organisational reality. People rarely experience work relationships as set out in organisational charts. In youth services, as in other organisations, these charts typically seem to confuse authority with status or grading, depicting structures such as the one represented in Figure 7.

These charts raise a number of important questions and give rise to assumptions which in practice cause great confusion for those occupying particular roles.

What, for example, do the lines connecting the various roles mean? Do they imply that one role holder is expected or authorised to issue instructions to others? In the example given, is the senior youth worker the manager of youth workers? Is the deputy principal youth officer the manager of area youth officers? Does the deputy principal have the right to appoint staff or to be involved in appointments? Who is involved in allocating duties or assigning specific areas of work? Who has

Key issues in youth service organisation 31

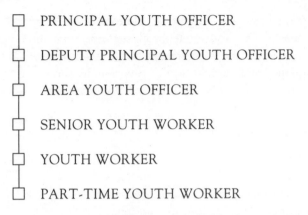

□ PRINCIPAL YOUTH OFFICER

□ DEPUTY PRINCIPAL YOUTH OFFICER

□ AREA YOUTH OFFICER

□ SENIOR YOUTH WORKER

□ YOUTH WORKER

□ PART-TIME YOUTH WORKER

Figure 7. *A typical youth service structure*

responsibility for furthering staff development or appraising performance? Who is involved in relation to decisions about unsatisfactory performance?

The project's work indicates that these issues are important in youth service organisation, and that official structures typically do not take into account the complexity and subtlety of the authority relationships that can exist. Youth service staff usually recognise where the posts of real responsibility or influence are located, even if this is often only an intuitive or implicit recognition. They are often acutely aware of superfluous managerial levels in their organisation. Where such superfluity is bound up with established work relationships, decision-making and accountability often become very hazy. In many situations it was found that accountability, in the sense of a creative relationship involving individuals in the mapping and reviewing of work, is replaced by conflict, confusion, and anxiety.

The familiar syndrome of people being 'left to get on with it' arises in these circumstances. This does not promote the realisation of creative potential in staff; nor does it contribute to the delivery of an effective service.

> *According to the chart and the staff development policy I'm supposed to be responsible for all the full-timers in the district. This seemed OK*

at first but now nobody seems sure about what's going on. I don't know whether I'm fully responsible for them at all ... It doesn't feel like it.

District youth and community officer

No, the district officer isn't really the manager. I see her more as an adviser to me anyway ... I use her as a sounding board and to help me if I need it with some of the problems that crop up in the work. There is an expectation we are responsible to her but it doesn't work out like that.

Youth and community worker

These examples begin to suggest some important ideas in the area of authority relationships. There is a clear recognition in the youth service of the need for line managerial roles, although their location and design is not always so clear. But the possibility of other types of authority relationship does not generally seem to have been explored in any depth. It is unnecessarily constraining on services and staff to think only in terms of full line managerial roles. The examples quoted above suggest a different kind of authority relationship involving a less intense degree of authority than that required of a line managerial relationship. The district officer's relationship with the youth and community worker seems to be about supporting, advising, and perhaps recommending particular courses of action to the worker. The main problem, especially for the officer, is a lack of clarity about this role: what is expected of this individual has not been adequately or accurately defined.

There is a view in the youth service that line managerial authority is the only legitimate kind of managerial authority, and that line managerial relationships are the only kind involving true accountability. This view oversimplifies organisational life and ignores the potential for a variety of managerial roles and relationships—and, in consequence, types or intensities of accountability. Again the reader is referred to Appendix 3, which identifies some different managerial types and their possible roles in the youth service.

One further dimension of youth service organisation in which authority relationships become particularly significant and a source of

Key issues in youth service organisation **33**

problems is that of the various committees which operate: unit management committees and district or area committees, for example. Project work suggests that these committees, particularly at unit level, are often clear about their technical functions (financial accounting, lettings, and building maintenance, for instance), yet problems seem to arise in relation to staffing matters. The main question seems to hinge on the type and level of authority that committees have in relation to both full-time and part-time staff. Are committees expected to issue instructions and give detailed programmes of work to staff? Are they expected or required to advise on, recommend, or decide the work of the unit? Are they expected to monitor or appraise the work of staff? And what degree of accountability do youth workers have in relation to their committees? Some quotations from the project's fieldwork begin to suggest the nature of the difficulties experienced. The following came from committee members interviewed in different project locations:

[The youth worker] is the professional and we let him get on with it.

I think it's the youth officer who decides on the youth worker's work. They impose their decisions and it doesn't matter what we say.

We couldn't decide what kind of work the staff do ... But they do report to us on management committees.

Things have got very difficult ... I don't really know who is in charge here. Is it us or the authority?

These remarks are typical of the confusions expressed by committee members. Too often committee work is left unspecified and the nature of committee authority and the corresponding accountability of staff is often ill-defined.

The project found that authority relationships are of great concern to those working in the youth service. These relationships influence everyone, from principal officers to part-time staff and volunteers. Clearly specified, they are crucial in binding organisations together and mapping out the expectations, requirements, and obligations that attach to work roles. Imprecisely or badly defined, they are a source of difficulty, conflict, and confusion, and can seriously limit and damage the work of the service.

Summary points

- It is important to distinguish between level of authority, grade, and status.
- Organisational charts rarely give a picture of organisational reality.
- The level of authority attached to a role must be specified: authority to do what with whom?
- Line managerial role relationships are critically important in ensuring that the work of the organisation and its members is specified.
- There is scope in youth services for authority relationships which do not carry full managerial responsibilities.
- The work and authority level of youth service committees needs careful thought and specification.

Work expectations and role specifications

Some roles in the youth service have grown or expanded in arbitrary and ill-considered ways. Some services appear to have been more concerned with attracting funding or grant aid for particular projects than with specifying the work of those projects and the roles required within them. While this may be understandable in a service that has suffered chronic underfunding for so long, the consequences of these developments cannot be ignored.

Roles which are poorly defined and jobs which are poorly specified have often just grown up around individuals. Project-based roles, sometimes initially funded from external sources, have often developed without any analysis of what concrete work is required of them. Unrealistic combinations of policy work, developmental work, and client contact work make it difficult for those in post to be clear about what is expected of them. The identification of real work demands much more than simply a requirement to deliver 'social education' in a particular location.

Project work suggests that youth service staff frequently undertake inappropriate and excessive amounts of work. Often they are expected to be all things to all people, and the formal expectation that they will deliver work at a particular level of impact is unrealistic. These expectations seem to fall on part-time staff or those with little experience as well as on more experienced staff:

> *I am a trainee in this authority and I think it is wrong that I should be expected to run this centre in the same way as a fully qualified youth worker. There have been several times when I felt that I was out of my depth and I don't think we get the support that we should.*
>
> Trainee youth and community worker

> *[The employing authority seems] to forget that we are part-time staff. They rely a lot on our good will to get the service run ... but I don't think we get the recognition we deserve. They seem to want us to do more and more but there is a point where you just can't do any more.*
>
> Part-time youth worker

There are also questions here concerning the match between individual capability and level of responsibility. Such questions have implications for selection and appointment. It is unrealistic to expect trainees or part-time staff to undertake the work normally undertaken by experienced and professionally qualified staff. The consequences of placing people in these positions are often serious, leading to the loss of skilled and talented individuals.

One particular situation in which a match between capability or potential and responsibility needs to be carefully thought out is that of the transition from fieldworker to youth officer—in work level terms, the transition between level-2 and level-3 work. Discussions with people in the field suggest that this raises particular problems, despite the commonplace assumption that good youth workers make good youth officers. The transition from level-2 to level-3 work demands a conceptual reorientation, and it must be carefully managed. The level-

3 work needs to be clearly identified and specified. Our work suggests that this is not always done, with youth officers often uncertain about their role and what is expected of them at this level. The individuals concerned sometimes manage this uncertainty and its inherent tensions by making an inappropriate return to level-2 work, even though there is an understanding that this is not what is expected of the youth officer. This situation is compounded by a prevalent view in youth services that the 'real' work of the organisation is that which is concerned with direct contact work at client level. While in one sense this is appropriate, it is very important that other types of work (planning, programming, scheduling, managing, supporting, and so on) are undertaken to support and extend work at client level. Properly established, youth officer roles are of critical importance in ensuring this.

Summary points

- It is essential when setting up projects to ensure that they are carefully specified in terms of purposes and roles and that they are established and managed at the appropriate work level.
- Work roles should be carefully and thoughtfully designed, rather than simply left to grow into unrealistic combinations of different levels of work.
- The responsibilities of individuals should be carefully matched with their capabilities.
- The transition between different levels of work needs careful management. The new work should be clearly specified, and any induction and training needs responded to.
- There is a need to recognise the importance of work other than direct client contact. The youth service needs its managerial roles.

Absence of clear policy

Discussions with youth service staff indicated that the concept of policy is slippery and elusive. There is consensus in the field that 'having a policy and knowing what it is' is important. But the reality seems to be that policy, as an expression of purpose, is often contradictory, ambiguous, unclear, or entirely absent:

> Nobody knows where we're supposed to be going here. There isn't a policy and it seems that you could do just about anything as long as you don't rock the boat or get the elected members involved.
>
> Youth worker

> What's the club here for? I don't know really ... To keep them occupied I suppose.
>
> Part-time youth worker

> We will work to a policy if we know what it is.
>
> Youth and community officer

The provision of explicit statements of purpose, on behalf of a particular youth service or unit, is essential to the delivery of services or programmes which are co-ordinated, purposeful, and amenable to monitoring and evaluation. Without policy it is difficult for an organisation to have much idea of its impact on the world, since without clear purposes there is little with which to compare outcomes.

Statements of purpose reflect the underlying values of the organisation. They inevitably include statements of what is believed to be good, appropriate, or important. In one sense, policy can be seen as the expression of values through purpose. As such, policy provides individuals with important opportunities to commit themselves to the organisation through sharing and upholding its values. These values give a sense of identity to the organisation and the individuals within it. In this way, coherent policy statements have an important integrating function.

Most importantly, policy sets a boundary around work. Many of the interviews undertaken on the project have shown that, in the absence of policy, youth service staff are unclear about direction or priority. It is easy in these circumstances to get into a situation where 'anything goes' and effective work happens by luck rather than design. By providing boundaries, policy can reduce uncertainty to a manageable level and free individuals to exercise judgment and discretion.

Service or unit policy should be expressed in the form of a statement, ideally agreed by all relevant parties, of organisational or unit purposes and the values which underlie them. And mechanisms for the review and development of policy need to be thought out. How often should the policy be reviewed? Who should be involved? Which views should the organisation take into account? Is the organisation's policy development a top-down or bottom-up process? In either case, is this appropriate?

Clear policy is essential, but it is not a panacea. In itself, a policy document is no more than a document, no more than text on a page. Its importance lies in how it can be used to map out work and create a sense of meaning for those engaged in that work.

Summary points

- Youth services and individual units or projects need clear and articulate statements of policy.
- Policy should express the organisation's purpose and values.
- No policy: no proper evaluation.
- Policy can foster integration in the organisation through shared values.
- Policy can set boundaries to the work.
- Policy reduces uncertainty, organisational and individual.
- Youth services need to establish appropriate mechanisms for policy formulation, review, and update.

6

Exploring youth work: the service–client interface

EACH of the project's research assistants was involved with two local authority youth services, and three different kinds of youth work situation were examined in each. A selection of the research material arising from this work will be presented in this chapter. Except where otherwise attributed, quotations are taken from the research assistants' field notes, and include further quotations from interviews.

Organising youth work staff

There is no doubt that the youth service relies heavily on its part-time staff. In all of the situations examined, there were full-time workers either managing or supporting groups of part-time staff. The exact nature of relations between full-time and part-time staff is not always clear to those involved. The appointment of a full-time district worker in one setting led to uncertainty about role relationships:

The part-time staff seem to be somewhat confused with this arrangement. 'We are unclear as to the full-time worker's role.' ... 'I don't think we see the district worker as part of our team ... There has not been enough working together.'

A major issue associated with the effectiveness of part-time staff teams related to support and supervision. Some teams seemed to work quite effectively without the strong involvement of a full-time worker; in others there was a sense of loss of direction:

The team is excellent because its members are committed and are willing to make the team excellent ... Each staff member is complementary to the others and this also contributes to the team's success.

Although the large majority of part-time workers with whom I have spoken expressed the same fears, complaints, and disillusionment about the work done at the centre, they all appeared to be ignorant of the fact that others among the staff group felt exactly the same.

Where full-time and part-time workers were involved in an effective team, the research assistant was 'pleasantly surprised at the amount of sharing of information which staff of the ... project did—both part-timers and full-timers'. In their own words, the staff saw the benefits of 'the linchpin that the full-time worker was becoming to the project: we are better informed about what is going on—here, there, and everywhere'.

Clearly, a cohesive staff team and effective communication between the full-time and part-time workers can be positive influences on the quality of work undertaken with young people:

The staff had enthusiasm and frequently turned that enthusiasm into practice. While I was present the staff decided a barbecue was to be held next week, the kids were eager, and the staff themselves organised the buying of the necessary provisions ... On another occasion, and presumably carried on after my stay, the idea of producing their annual magazine came up. One member of staff initiated the work in this area, providing the necessary materials and equipment, and the members were able to come and write anything they felt was necessary.

All staff ... seemed to offer something tangible to the club. One was artistic and could draw posters and help with the magazine, one was good at snooker and sports so could contribute something there,

another was able to coach table tennis, another was a canoe expert ...
Accompanied by the general enthusiasm of the staff it made a very
able and productive team.

This may not always follow, however:

The interaction with the members is restricted to a minimal level and
on an 'only if necessary' basis. Most evenings the staff frequent either
the office or the coffee bar on a regular basis. There have been in fact
evenings during which staff members remained in those areas for an
entire session. On another occasion, and during an evening session,
the staff sat chatting around one table in the socialising area, and
almost, it seemed, avoiding the members.

Summary points

- The role of full-time youth and community workers and team
  leaders, particularly in relation to their teams of part-time staff,
  should be clearly spelled out.
- The work expected of part-time staff should be clearly defined.
- Part-time and voluntary workers should be given regular support and
  supervision.
- Clubs and centres should have a fully planned programme related to
  the needs of the members. Help with planning and back-up support
  from the staff operating at work level 2 is essential if the youth
  service curriculum is to be innovative and relevant.

Work with clients

Project experience confirms that there is confusion about the nature of
social education. For example:

We fall into the education bracket and not social services. I guess you
must have heard words like ... 'we are social educationalists'. The
word is bandied about so much I'm not altogether too sure what it
means myself.

Part-time youth worker

Even when there was some understanding of social education, there tended to be quite a gulf between the explicit purposes of the youth service, as embodied in policy statements, and the same purposes as interpreted by the service's professional staff, whether officers or workers:

Social education is not seen as any sort of formalised education. Social education is a mode, a mode of thinking—a form of understanding, a mode of working with young people. It needn't be as most people see it, a heavy conicaled [sic] working process. It should flow, it should be an easy thing ... Social education is dependent upon ... the staff—staffing—the ability of those staff to be aware of what they are doing and how they are doing it. At present—yes there are certain members of staff—and I would include myself—who are aware of those things when they talk to kids and when they are entering relationships or conversations with kids ... Allowing the young people to get something out of it more than just the mere action and learn by certain things.

Full-time youth worker

There is a parallel gulf between the service's perceptions of itself and, on the other hand, the way it is perceived by its clients:

Our members seem to have a different view of what all this is about. Most of us talk about social education. The members go on about pool and table tennis. I don't think this is necessarily a problem, because we can effectively work in these areas.

Full-time worker

Young people's expectations of the service were very limited, and often did not match the aspirations of workers. They might come to youth clubs and centres to meet friends, to engage in some activity, or simply because they had nothing else to do.

I only come here at the start of the week. On the other days I go drinking. I just come here when I haven't got any money. The trouble is, it's a quid to get down to town and a quid to get back. I don't mind it here, mind. It's just a bit boring.

Youth centre member

Exploring youth work: the service–client interface **43**

I've been coming here with me mates for about six months now. I used to be too involved with judo. I do come for some of the activities like football and badminton and that. Mainly just to see me mates. It's good here—well worth the money.

Youth club member

Many claims are made regarding the effectiveness of youth work. Youth workers have a strong belief that the work they undertake, and their interventions with young people, are effective and worthwhile and likely to have a major influence on young people's development and future adult lives. And yet there seems to be little work undertaken in youth services to investigate or substantiate such claims. These uncritically optimistic beliefs and perceptions seem, for youth workers and their managers, sufficient in themselves as evidence for effective intervention:

I think it is just a feeling you get when you talk to them. It is difficult to define I know. But still valid I think.

Full-time youth worker

Research indicates that youth workers often believe their claims to success to be, in principle, untestable:

No, I don't think we really know whether we are effective or not. We can look at attendance figures, and whether people do well in sport or find jobs. Otherwise we can only go on what members say to us, the general atmosphere of the centre.

Part-time youth worker

Attempts to define outcomes or success are frequently bedevilled by arguments about the importance of *process*. Our view is that these arguments are often unnecessary diversions, concealing a fundamental absence of clear purposes and intentions for youth work.

Far more attention should, in our view, be given to demonstrating the outcomes of youth work intervention. This will require clearly defined purposes, agreed criteria of effectiveness, and the appropriate means for making evaluative judgments. The youth service must, if it

44 *Youth service management*

is to sustain any position in public service and welfare provision, be able to provide a coherent account of its own principles, purposes, and outcomes. This must reflect the good practice which undoubtedly exists, in contrast to other instances of *ad hoc* and inadequately formulated work.

If fundamental purposes are to be clarified, the service must ask itself the simplest questions. For example, when young people walk into a youth centre for the first time:

- What is the youth service going to do for them?
- How long will it take?
- How will the service or its workers know whether they have been successful?

Social education is seen by many as the *raison d'être* of the youth service and the principle underlying the range of activities which comprise its curriculum. But for a variety of reasons youth service provision often fails to serve the ends of social education, or does so only haphazardly, sometimes allowing activities to become an end in themselves rather than a vehicle for youth work.

For example, the Management and Development Project visited an Action Sport project which was very well equipped and included in its range of activities weight training, swimming, squash, indoor soccer, basketball, indoor bowls, archery, rifle shooting, table tennis, pool, badminton, water sports, canoeing, sub-aqua, diving, judo, football, cricket, golf, cycling, women's keep-fit, darts, cards, and board games. Many of these activities were provided for up to five days a week. But the conditions under which staff were recruited, under the aegis of the Manpower Services Commission, meant that it was not always possible to provide expert coaching, and workers often seemed to rely on the skills and knowledge of the clients themselves. The project lacked skilled staff who could instruct others in how the equipment should be used. There are safety factors here too.

I'm supposed to help with the weights but I don't know anything about it. We are never put in our current sports.

MSC worker

Exploring youth work: the service–client interface **45**

The staff are not professionally trained. [The public] ask if we could train them—but we can't. If we had trained people it would encourage them to come.

MSC worker

The staff should have more interest in it and know about it. You just have to look around—you can see that most have no idea what they are doing. They don't know anything about muscles.

Client

The job description of the full-time worker in this situation was to 'provide a balanced programme of sport and recreation activities for people living within each of the authority's areas, with particular emphasis on working with individuals and groups who were not involved in sport and recreational activities'. With a project of this kind, there is inevitably a question of staff training—whether it is activity skills or social education that is needed.

In a centre-based situation in another authority, the problem was not poor staff training but the simple *substitution* of sports facilities for youth work:

The activities undertaken at the centre and the size and integration of its membership appear unreasonably limited. The sporting activities on offer—football, badminton, cricket, basketball—would seem to appeal to a partial membership. Those who use the centre for a specific reason, such as a sport, undertake that activity immediately on arrival, possibly purchase a drink afterwards, and leave promptly. There is only a small handful of members (less than ten) who could be judged to be using the centre regularly on an other-than-ends-oriented basis. In this sense, the centre appears little more than a recreational hall, a sports centre—which, when compared to the overall purpose of the authority's service, is a far cry from the explicit goal.

In another authority there was clearly a belief in social education, but low staffing levels reduced the impact of what could be offered. The members' interest in the centre did not revolve around its activities and facilities; but neither did they come for social education:

They picked out particular members of staff who they liked to talk to, and friends who they came to meet. Most of the members ... appeared to view the centre chiefly as a place to meet in the evenings, a social centre.

The staff were aware of the need to introduce more structured social activities into the centre. Contact with members was decidedly informal—comments in passing, brief conversations at the entrance table, and so on ... Opportunities appear to have been missed, largely through wholly inadequate levels of staffing, a problem of which all staff appeared to be acutely aware.

What goes on in centres is in some cases only tenuously related to social education. There is always the question of *balance* related to the programme for a centre. Is the programme too activity-oriented, at the expense of a response to other needs? Does it respond in a relevant way to the needs of particular groups of young people—girls and young women, for example? Over time, norms become established, influenced particularly by full-time staff. Take, for instance, this youth wing:

In constant use, the largest room within the youth wing comprises four pool tables, two dartboards, two table-tennis tables, and two loudspeakers through which current chart music is played. Seating is organised around these pieces of equipment. The coffee bar is a smaller room, next to the entrance of the wing, consisting of a sweets and drinks counter, a drinks vending machine, and a television, around which most of the chairs are organised. For those who require a quieter space than is offered here, there are an additional two rooms at the back of the wing, containing tables and chairs. The club has additional use of relevant school premises, such as the swimming pool, the gym, tennis courts, and hard courts (used for cricket). A hairdressing salon has been set up in the girls' lavatory; classes are run by an activity leader who has worked as a hairdresser. There is also a cupboard/room which is used as a makeshift darkroom for occasional photography sessions run either by a volunteer or by the full-time leader. Members are notified, via the noticeboard, of district social and sports events, for which they are usually charged money for the journey.

The full-time worker in this youth wing placed less emphasis on activities than his predecessor, and professed support for participation by members. In his own words:

> The ideal, although it would never happen, would be for the kids to be able to take over my job ... This comes back to relationships between people, to enabling kids to do things, and myself and my staff supporting them in that ...

When some of the senior members suggested the establishment of a members' committee, he initially supported the venture:

> I said, 'Yes, OK, if you're quite certain what's going to happen and you are quite positive about how it's going to form ... go ahead.'

However, he subsequently contradicted himself by withdrawing his support, apparently feeling that a committee was likely to cause friction between those members sitting on it and those not:

> In my terms it's something that has never been on ... I came back from holiday last year and some people said, 'We've got a members' committee.' ... Now I wasn't happy about that and I showed I wasn't happy by not supporting it. But I wasn't going to say 'no way'.

As a result of all this, there was general confusion. Some members thought they still had a committee; the full-time leader was still expected by members to function in a way which he clearly found unacceptable. Because of the misunderstanding, planned events and ideas were seldom realised. This tension raised questions not only as to how strategies of participation might be incorporated into the club but also of communication, which appeared to have been the barrier between intention and realisation on this and further occasions.

Summary points

- There is a need for all staff, both full-time and part-time, paid and voluntary, to understand the term *social education*.
- What counts as success in youth work should be articulated by the youth service.

- Training can contribute to the clarification of social education and the articulation of the body of knowledge which underlies youth work.
- Staffing levels should be examined to ensure that the expected work can be undertaken effectively.
- There is a need for more positive and purposeful youth work.
- Opportunities for client participation should be exploited.

The full-time youth work role

Full-time youth workers are formally employed for ten sessions a week, one session comprising a morning, afternoon, or evening. It is clear from the evidence which has emerged from the project that different workers make different interpretations of how these sessions should be used, particularly in the amount of face-to-face work undertaken during a typical week. Fieldwork notes will be drawn on in order to characterise different patterns of work. First, the range of work undertaken by particular workers is exemplified in extracts from three shadowing accounts written by the project's research assistants.

Account 1

There are certain disadvantages in being the full-time worker in this small town. Owing to the size of the community and the fact that the worker lives locally, she has a high profile and is always 'on call'. In effect, there are no set hours. The busiest parts of the day, however, are always mornings and evenings, with a slightly lighter programme during the afternoons.

During the morning the worker is usually engaged with the administration of the centre. This responsibility includes paperwork, visits to the bank, weekly visits to the area youth office, and liaison with new members of the organisation using the premises. Often, however, she spends morning sessions organising, advertising, or seeking support for various ongoing events and activities. An example of such a morning session could be the handing out of leaflets advertising the playscheme at local schools. During mornings, the worker is visited by individual members who need special counselling or information. This is often extremely time-consuming, so that administration and the like is sometimes left for the afternoon.

Also during mornings, the full-time worker is often engaged in a type of detached youth work at a local café frequented by youths not attending the centre and to whom she offers counselling and information.

Afternoons are not so heavily scheduled. Usually they are used for preparing the club for the evening session or for catching up with work left over from the busy morning session.

The evening session involves supervision of the overall programme taking place in the club and the counselling of members. The interaction with the members is frequent and regular. At the end of the evening the worker prepares the administrative material—daysheets, subs, coffee-bar money, and so on—for the next morning's work.

This schedule is often varied by the worker's attendance at meetings or by the supervisory sessions that she provides to another club which is run by part-time staff.

Account 2

The day for the full-time worker in the youth wing begins at 10.00 a.m. and ends 12 hours later when the club closes. A 'normal' day involves arrival at the club at around 10.00 a.m., often after a visit to the area youth office for the collection of mail. In most cases, from that time until lunch the worker is engaged in administration and paperwork relating to the club or in the correction and preparation of the homework assigned to her geography class pupils. Three mornings a week she is teaching until 12.00 noon, and two of those days also involve revision classes in the early afternoon.

At noon, the club is open to the fifth-years as a socialising area. The full-time worker assumes supervisory duties for the time during which the pupils are in the club—that is, until 1.15 p.m.

In the afternoons, when she is not teaching, the worker continues with administration and school work, taking a one-hour break before the evening club. Often the unemployed youngsters come in during the afternoon and take advantage of the fact that the full-time worker is there. On Thursday afternoons she attends a counselling and communication course in a local town.

Although this represents a typical day at the youth wing, the routine is sometimes altered by daytime meetings or by duties which emerge out of special ongoing activities. There have been occasions, for example, when the worker had to visit nearby schools to liaise with them on specific events such as festivals or weekends.

Overall, this full-time worker is a stranger to the notion of a ten-session week. Owing to her teaching and school responsibilities, the involvement which the club has established within the community, and her youth work duties, she is always busy.

Account 3

The full-time worker's day is divided into three main parts. The morning session starts at 10.00 a.m. and ends around 2.30 p.m. From Monday to Thursday an MSC project is in operation during this time. The full-time worker supervises the MSC workers during these sessions as well as organising club matters in general. The supervision work entails close co-operation and facilitates the use of the centre by the project workers. The project has not achieved its original objectives, and as a result the amount of supervision received has been somewhat less than had been envisaged, now making only relatively minor demands on the youth worker's time. During my three-week placement, much of the worker's time was taken up with making arrangements to install an alarm system in the club. The task of getting quotations from various companies proved to be very time-consuming, especially as it entailed visits from company representatives.

In the mornings the worker often visits the area youth office to collect or return the minibus or to collect mail and information. Friday mornings are used to update and file the club's daysheets, to arrange the financial side of the club, including the processing of pay sheets, and *to deal with lettings and membership matters. On one occasion the worker visited another full-time worker to make arrangements for a district competition.*

The afternoon session, 2.30 to 7.00 p.m., is usually time off for the worker, with only rare exceptions. There are weekly visits to the bank to deposit or withdraw money, and frequently to pay equipment or maintenance bills. Visits to the local Co-op to buy stock for the coffee bar are also included in afternoon periods.

The third part of the day, 7.00 to 10.00 p.m., is the time of the youth club. During these periods the worker has minimal contact with members and is usually there in a supervisory capacity. Interaction with staff members is also part of his role. He often collects subscriptions and hands out equipment requested by the members (pool cues, bats, and so on). Another part of his normal activities is the close supervision and preparation of the sports hall, which is used by outside groups as well as by club members. He is also the main keyholder, and therefore responsible for the final check at closing time.

These illustrations raise questions about how full-time youth workers use their time, whether they use it effectively, and whether some of the tasks they undertake could be better organised or more appropriately performed by ancillary clerical workers or others. Low-level administrative tasks can eat into the time available for other work:

The centre employs its own part-time clerical assistant, who handles substantial amounts of paperwork. Yet the time of the full-time centre manager is also largely spent largely fulfilling administrative duties, at times to the exclusion of all else.

This centre manager was expected to undertake the supervision of part-time staff as an integral element of 'personal development', but there was little evidence that any such sessions had taken place in recent months. As one part-time worker complained: 'Supervision is for feedback on an equal basis ... We rarely have these sessions—I haven't had one for about sixteen months. I think we should have a session about once a term.'

How do the various components of the full-time youth work role fit together, and what proportions of each type of work are necessary for effective work at client level? How much time should youth workers spend working face-to-face? How much of their time should be devoted to management or administration? How much to planning the work of the unit or project? And, importantly, who decides all this?

Summary points

- There is a need to be clearer about the range of tasks expected of youth workers and time balance during a typical week. Thought should be given to the time allocation for such duties as:
  —administration, including banking and purchasing;
  —liaison with individuals and organisations;
  —service and area meetings;
  —face-to-face work with clients;
  —support and training of staff;
  —project work;
  —personal training and development.
- Full-time workers should be encouraged to examine the range of tasks to be accomplished and explore the scope for delegation.

Inter-agency co-operation and liaison

The project's work revealed an enormous and sometimes bewildering range of liaison and contacts between the youth service and other agencies, statutory and voluntary. At youth officer level and above, many relationships with other sections and departments of the local authority and other agencies were acknowledged to be informal, and contact seemed to be made on a 'when necessary' basis. With some of the mainstream departments and agencies—social services and probation, for example—contacts existed through a number of joint projects with which the youth services were involved. Working parties considering issues of corporate concern (such as vandalism or street disturbances) also provided an opportunity for the youth service to contribute alongside other professionals. At officer level, youth service involvement with other agencies also occurred through police liaison committees and community relations councils. In all the participating authorities, partnership arrangements with the voluntary sector had been established and liaison was in progress.

At unit or centre level, contacts were equally wide-ranging, with evidence of joint work suggesting that useful liaison was taking place between youth workers and other professionals. Examples included involvement on MSC schemes, membership of liaison committees, and individual contact between different agency professionals regarding clients.

In general there was no clear pattern of liaison and contact which was common to the six youth services taking part in the project. Liaison occurred partly as a result of personal interest and investment by individual personnel. This can lead to effective joint work, but such arrangements are vulnerable to staff turnover.

Summary points

- Services should realistically identify the potential for joint work where a combined approach is likely to result in a positive response to client need.
- Liaison and inter-agency work should be purposeful.
- The potential inconsistency between different professional value systems should be taken into account when planning liaison work.
- It is necessary to consider the implications of work levels in relation to the membership of joint working groups.
- Effective inter-agency co-operation requires agreed policy formulations established by all parties concerned.

7

Outcomes and responses

*B*Y the end of 1986, the main programme of fieldwork on the project had been completed and summaries of this work presented to the LPMGs. They gave an initial consideration to the implications of this research for their services. Early in 1987 the first of two conferences was held at Brunel, and members of the six LPMGs were invited to meet together to review progress and to consider the next stage of the project's work, which would be concerned with the management of change.

During the conference discussions it was emphasised that the LPMGs were non-executive bodies and as such would need to act as catalysts in raising issues for consideration at various levels within their youth services and, more generally, the education departments in which those services operate. Clearly, some issues could be handled by the youth service itself—for example, support structures for members of staff. Others, like the need for restructuring or the appointment of a new youth officer, would require senior management and committee approval, since such change was likely to require the allocation of resources which might not be achieved for several years.

The project organised a second LPMG conference, one year after the first, which considered the relationship between organisational change and levels of work. This assisted LPMGs in further refining strategies for change in their organisations.

In the light of the issues raised by the initial fieldwork, and consideration of more theoretical issues at the conferences, LPMGs subsequently planned quite diverse programmes of work. Each of them identified a number of key areas of work which derived from the fieldwork programme. Five of the six LPMGs wrote covering reports detailing the issues to be worked on in their authorities. These reports also suggested ways in which the issues might be approached and were used by LPMGs in presentations to staff groups and politicians. This was part of the process of dissemination of the project's work, and aimed to stimulate and encourage a wider ownership of the need for change.

Reflections by heads of service

The heads of all six participating youth services were invited to provide written feedback about the project at the end of the third year. They were asked to reflect on the usefulness of the project to their work and their service, and to identify any particular problems which had arisen in the course of the work. The main points of this feedback are presented below, with quotations from the written responses.

The operation of the LPMGs

For most of the participating services the establishment of a group made up of officers and workers from all levels of their organisations, and especially for a project of this kind, was unique. One officer described the LPMG as 'an enthusiastic, energetic, committed group of youth workers concerned not only about young people but about improving the service to young people'. The same officer continued:

> The unique composition of the LPMG has demonstrated how communications across the service can be improved, that the issues arising from the research are owned universally, and that the involvement of all levels of worker can be valued.

One of the authorities had used a similar type of group to draw up its staff development policy, and therefore had warm expectations of the LPMG: 'Staff expected that, once the project was underway, it would prove to be a positive way to move forward.'

However, there were some alleged difficulties in the operation of two LPMGs:

> *Some problems were experienced in the honouring of the confidentiality promised to staff involved in the research interviews where LPMG members were reporting back and keeping colleagues in their staff team conversant with the progress being made.*

> *The LPMG ... did not always operate within its terms of reference ... The members of the LPMG began to attempt to negotiate with the director on behalf of workers within the service.*

The latter incident led to several meetings between project staff and authority officers, and subsequently the director of education. It was clear that within this authority there were proposals for major change being planned by elected members, apparently with little consultation— a situation likely to give rise to a sense of discontinuity. Members of the LPMG became particularly disturbed by this, and felt that project documents should be brought to the attention of councillors and the director of education. This placed the head of service, who was a member of the LPMG, in a difficult position. He had divided loyalties in his capacity as an officer of the authority and a member of the LPMG. These difficulties had not been fully resolved by the time the project ended.

Two of the six authorities were being subjected to new policy formulations at different stages of the project. In one there was 'continuous and sometimes radical change ... caused by a number of changes in political control'. Such changes led to a feeling of powerlessness within these two LPMGs. Despite this, however, the LPMGs worked effectively and were able to process the issues raised from the interviews into strategies for action.

Attitudes to the project

I had hitherto considered management to be about motivating people by giving them space to make decisions for themselves, about engaging with them in some teamwork exercise to enable them to share in the formulation of policy and thereby influence the service. I eschewed line management as denying what I perceived as good youth work practice, which was to make all in the service autarchic and self-reliant. I had a self-image as the principal youth worker, rather than the principal youth officer, and wanted to retain a flexible and sensitive approach which enhanced spontaneity ...

When the findings were made known to me, I was, at first, a little shocked. Some of the sacred cows ... were challenged and threatened. Policy needed to be articulated—not by word of mouth when the mood suited or the occasion demanded, but in writing—and available to all. Greater clarity was needed ... I was made painfully aware, whereas I thought most people had access to the information, that in the main it resided in my head, and often required my presence either to articulate it chapter and verse or to give some interpretation of it. While I perceived this lack of clarity as providing a measure of freedom to others, I realise that this was a chimera as lack of such information actually depowered [sic] those others and ensured that in practice the power resided with me and me alone.

This principal youth officer's attitude speaks for itself. But it became evident that, despite careful initial negotiation of the ground rules for the project and an explanation of the methods to be adopted, some heads of service expected it to provide a service evaluation where 'good points' would be juxtaposed with the 'bad'. This expectation, and the attitude to which it led, seemed to the researchers to have markedly inhibited the encouragement they gave to the LPMG, despite the fact that they themselves were members. Project staff were made aware that youth service staff in more than one of the authorities were being accused of disloyalty for raising issues of concern through the project.

The intention was that the issues raised in the project should be viewed by the LPMGs as agenda items for consideration, not as a series of recommendations drawn out by the researchers. Some heads of service appreciated this:

> As issues being explored by the research within the county became clearer, there were indications that the ways of addressing these issues would require major changes within the service. These were likely to include delivery, structures, management, and communication.

Others did not:

> The process of analysis resulted in a set of recommendations that were not as clear as they might have been, did not address all the issues, and did not give clear directions for further action. This was, in part, a consequence of the make-up of the LPMG. The final recommendations were a synthesis of the many different perspectives of future actions.

In one county authority the project's work immediately followed a major review of the youth service, and strengthened 'previous cases for change':

> The consequences of this have been a defensive stance in certain quarters of the service to the negative issues raised by the results of the research project.

The interface work undertaken by the research assistant gave cause for concern in another authority:

> A major difficulty arose ... This was clearly a very important part of the research, designed to examine the effectiveness of the service in meeting the needs of young people ... The research in fact was purely anecdotal, highlighted the gossip and rumour, produced no evidence for a number of outrageous conclusions, and was fundamentally inaccurate. In the absence of this vital link in the project it is difficult to evaluate the effectiveness of the service.

The composite report was subsequently withdrawn at the authority's request after its presentation to the LPMG. The report reflected important undercurrents in the service's culture and aspects of its structure, organisation, and operation. Workers on the LPMG were more willing to accept it than senior managers, who responded by rejecting it as poorly presented research. The interview material which informed the report indicated that there were many individual bones to pick, which when openly discussed became shared bones, revealing underlying dissatisfaction with the service and its operation. The rejection of the report meant that very real issues about how the youth service workforce felt were left unattended.

Resourcing

Major research such as that of the Management and Development Project inevitably depended on the good will of the authorities in releasing staff for interviews and for involvement in the LPMG. In two authorities additional paid support was provided for the LPMG, in one case for the whole of the three-year period and in another for approximately a year. In another authority secretarial help was made available.

> Evidence over the whole period shows many hundreds of staff hours spent and a budget allocation on an increasing scale from Year 1 to the end of the project. This figure was in excess of £5,500 for the final year of the project, to pay for additional sessions and travelling.

Achievements and future developments

> The process stimulated staff at all levels to examine the delivery of the service to young people in a collaborative and positive way. Action has been taken on a number of minor matters identified by the LPMG and plans for the implementation of the major issues are being finalised.

The changes proposed in one authority were very extensive, the project having led to the preparation of a 'major restructuring report', subsequently used for consultation with staff as a prelude to implementation. However, even the smallest changes, if they enhance the effectiveness of the service, will have been worthwhile.

[Staff] need clear parameters in which to operate and their absence hinders autonomy … I am now confident that, together with all those who share my aspirations for a vibrant and dynamic youth service in the borough, we can devise and implement strategies for change which address those deficiencies that the research has revealed.

Ultimately, the project was concerned with the quality of service delivery, and some heads of service understood this:

The project came within the context of review of the service, and the evidence produced clearly supported the need for such a review and indeed supported a number of proposals that were being considered … Much of the work that was done by the researcher in examining issues to do with management and development of the youth service contributed to the understanding of workers within the borough of the processes involved in improving the quality of the service … Overall the experience has been a difficult one but not totally without benefit.

The aim of the service is being debated and clarified; 'empowering young people' is becoming owned by all involved.

[We are] moving towards an improved service for and with young people, and the Brunel research project has been a significant factor in implementing this change.

It has been suggested by some heads of participating services that the Brunel Training Consultative Unit should undertake a full review of the outcomes of the project after a period of five years. This we should be pleased to undertake. We envisage that the review would highlight and evaluate changes that have occurred in participating services, identify examples of good practice, and determine where change has been blocked or found difficult to enact. Such evaluation would provide useful experience-based guidelines for the future organisation and management of change in youth services.

8

Conclusions, implications, and recommendations

M UCH of the work of the Brunel Management and Development
Project has long-term implications for the services involved. It is
difficult to gauge at this point the consequences of change already
proposed or enacted. Work in one authority suggested a need for quite
fundamental restructuring of the youth and community service, as was
recognised in subsequent proposals for change. Inevitably the
consequences of these changes will become evident only after a period
of some time. Review and evaluation of change will need careful
planning, and will be undertaken in different ways by the participating
services. Groups similar to the originally constituted LPMGs may well
provide a useful and effective arena for discussion. Indeed, they would
be able to undertake the crucial function of reviewing organisational
life more widely—examining and, where necessary, challenging the
basic policies, norms, and ways of operating that structure the
organisation's activities. They would also be able to stimulate wide
discussion and encourage innovation. These groups could take on an
unusually significant role in relation to planned change, and indeed a
number of the services involved in the project have decided to sustain
their LPMGs under a different nomenclature with a view to their
undertaking this further work.

Managing change

The 1987 LPMG conference focused on change by suggesting that it could not be seen as a basic concept on its own, but rather only in terms of the complementary relationship between change and constancy. These are not opposites, nor one good and the other bad. They make sense only when viewed together. Essentially, the management of organisational change is a matter of managing the relationship between change and constancy.[1]

In the management of change, there are three essential dimensions of an organisation to take account of:

* Purposes
* Activity
* Structures of meaning

Purposes are specific to a particular organisation and are determined by policy-makers. Examples of youth and community services' purposes might be to provide social education for young people, to give support and help to young people experiencing difficulties, or to help local communities meet the educational needs of their members. Purposes need to be transformed into programmes of *activity*: establishing a range of provision, working with particular groups, setting up specific projects. The third element is *structures of meaning*: the ways in which people understand and make sense of the work they are engaged in and how it is undertaken. Here, managers must appreciate the need to establish consensus, and a collective understanding not only of the present situation but of what individuals should be striving towards in their work.

The reduction of anxiety and stress is important in managing change, since individuals will need to feel comfortable, fully committed, and part of the change process. Some worry and anxiety is an inevitable

[1] We are indebted to Gillian Stamp for her ideas on the management of change, which have stimulated our own thinking and that of staff in the authorities participating in the project. Readers interested in pursuing the subject further should refer to G. Stamp, *The Management of Change*, Uxbridge, Brunel Training Consultative Unit, 1987, and *Some Further Thoughts on the Management of Change*, Uxbridge, Brunel Training Consultative Unit, 1988.

and necessary part of people's working through the issues and new expectations involved in the process of change, but such stresses should be kept to a minimum. LPMGs were urged to carefully prepare the ground for change before moving into the later phases of facilitation. Three kinds of change were identified:

- Improvement
- Growth
- Discontinuity

Improvement is concerned with extension—extending the existing purposes and structures of meaning, by making improvements to the work that is already occurring. Improvement involves doing more effectively what is already being done. *Growth* is concerned with taking on new areas of work which expand the range and responsibilities of an organisation. It might involve new projects and new approaches to the work of a service, unit, or project. *Discontinuity* is usually less controllable and leads to radical shifts in the purposes and activities of the organisation. One example of this might be the absorption of a youth service into a leisure department, or the appointment of a new head of service with fundamentally different ideas about how the service should be run. Discontinuity may lead to a sense of loss or disorientation, and may even be likened to a form of bereavement.

Some changes can be enacted swiftly, whereas others might take several years. The project has emphasised the need for a schedule of change to be considered alongside change mechanisms. When change is being planned or enacted, it is also important to be clear about who should be consulted and what form the consultation should take. Some individuals may be directly affected by the change envisaged, and may need to be helped to identify and 'own' these changes.

During the process of change, and even after agreement has been reached about new purposes and activities, it is important that some form of feedback loop is structured into the monitoring system. New purposes can become clouded when individuals say 'I hadn't realised it meant that.' It is also particularly important to be clear about change in relation to individuals' expected work level.

Social analysis and change

The formal end of a project provides a useful opportunity for reflecting on the various aspects of the work completed. We have reached the view that social analysis is a powerful means of organisational analysis which can lead to enactable change. In effect, it enables the members of an organisation to stand back and think about what is happening. It provides a space for review and reflection. As Gillian Stamp puts it, social analysis transforms 'what everyone knows'—perhaps implicitly or tacitly—into part of the common stock of knowledge.[2] This transformation opens up the possibility of:

- reducing unnecessary uncertainty and releasing energy wasted on it;
- laying bare uncertainties which offer challenge and attuning energy towards them;
- creating a common language which allows disciplined discussion of the constraints and opportunities that surround the work to be done;
- creating a body of knowledge which allows learning by reviewing experience that has been organised into a coherent pattern;
- creating, testing, and refining theories about the organisation of work.

The process of transformation is referred to as *clarification*. The project has contributed to this process in participating authorities by offering analysis of organisational problems and introducing concepts and theories where appropriate. Our experience strongly indicates that the need for organisational change emerges through the review of current policy and practice using the process described. By making implicit elements of an organisation explicit, social analysis reveals possibilities for the development of the organisation and its work.

The project's work suggests an ambivalent response to anticipated change. On the one hand there is the sense of excitement associated with new possibilities; on the other hand, and simultaneously, there may be a sense of anxiety about an unknown future. Essentially this is the duality of constancy and change referred to earlier. The social

[2] G. Stamp, 'A note on social analysis', unpublished, 1987.

analytic approach engages with the relationship between constancy and change, working closely with organisation members and helping them to disentangle their purposes, their activities, and the ways in which they make sense of these. Social analysis makes it possible to reconstruct these three components in the light of the need for change. A sense of ownership is developed on the part of organisation members, and thus a commitment to the implementation of change. Without such commitment, the most effective change is unlikely to occur.

Importantly, social analysis acknowledges the need for different kinds of change: improvement, growth, and discontinuity. It indicates that different kinds of change might need to occur at different organisational levels, and that a range of responses might need to be considered and planned.

Our work indicates that the social analytic method is profoundly empowering for organisation members, as it enables them to identify and engage with the real issues. As we have pointed out, this presents potential dangers if organisation members are not aware of the possible consequences of the approach. Nevertheless, social analysis holds considerable promise for organisational development in youth and community services.

Finally, to conclude this report, a series of principal recommendations have been drawn from the work undertaken over the three years of the project. Presented in three categories, these are addressed to government, local authorities (particularly education departments), and to youth and community services and their individual units and projects.

PRINCIPAL RECOMMENDATIONS

Policy

1 Government has a duty to fully articulate at a national level what it expects of the youth service within the available resources. This may require the precise definition of limits, so that youth work can become more sharply focused.

2 Local authorities, through the appropriate department, should be clear about the level of impact required of the youth service, and provide the appropriate space in terms of structure and resources for effective planning and delivery.

3 Youth services should articulate an appropriate written policy for their work, and ensure that it provides a relevant basis for planning and undertaking required work.

4 Areas, clubs, centres, and projects operating within the broad policy framework of the local authority youth service should formulate statements of policy which take account of local circumstances and conditions.

5 It is essential that statements of policy and purpose at any level are subject to regular review. The review process needs to take account of all relevant interests and perspectives within the service, including those of young people, and these need to be appropriately located within the political context of the service.

6 Given the youth service's commitment to equal opportunities, it is important to ensure that women, black people, and people with disabilities are properly represented in middle and senior management positions.

Work and management

1 It must be recognised that well-thought-out managerial practices are essential to the delivery of an effective service. Management, as an issue, should not be allowed to become yet another passing youth service whim. Youth services need to take time to reflect on their own managerial and organisational practices, and where necessary modify them.

2 Managers must recognise the different kinds of work necessary for the effective operation of a service. These correspond to the levels of work identified in the report.

3 Work levels are interdependent, and represent discrete management roles which contribute to the effective operation of a service. There is a sense in youth services that the only 'real' work is direct-contact

Conclusions, implications, and recommendations   67

work with clients. This can lead to the undermining of support, managerial, and development work. Service operation may need reviewing in the light of this.

4 Services need to exercise restraint in increasing the number of managerial levels. (The various consequences of installing pseudo-managerial roles are referred to in Chapter 5.)

5 It is important that services recognise the proper degree of discretion attached to particular roles and ensure that the appropriate resources are made available to those occupying these roles.

6 Services need to recognise that managerial roles and role relationships are not always of a line managerial kind. Others include monitoring, co-ordinating, and supervising roles which may be necessary for the proper support and development of the work of the service.

7 It is for managers to direct the transformation of policy into practice and provide the appropriate support. They should be assisted in this by others, when necessary.

8 Effective work with clients requires an appropriate allocation of resources and, in particular, a realistic ratio of staff to clients.

Development

1 Full-time youth workers should be seen as having full managerial responsibilities, within properly prescribed limits, in relation to part-time staff, trainees, resources, budget, and allocation of time. This has major implications for initial training and for support, especially during the probationary period.

2 The transition from centre or project worker to youth officer needs to be underpinned by in-service training and support related to the management requirements of the new level of work.

3 The resolution of many of the management issues identified in the project could be assisted by in-service training or consultancy, and GEST monies could greatly assist in this process. It may well be appropriate that this be identified as a national priority area in the future.

Appendix 1

Procedural sequence of the project

Contact and discussion with PYO or head of service
▼
Negotiation with CEO or representative
(PYO in attendance)
▼
Memorandum of agreement for service to become a client
▼
Definition of service policy
▼
Meeting with staff team
▼
Appointment of local project management group (LPMG)
▼
Identification of potential interviewees
▼
Agreement to interview, followed by interviews
▼
Clearance of written records to go to LPMG
▼
Material received and discussed by LPMG, and ◄───┐
papers cleared for wider dissemination │
▼   FEEDBACK
LOOP
Preparation of theoretical statements, ───────┘
papers, and generalisations
▼
Theoretical material made available to project steering group
and to seminars and conferences
▼
Project report and book

Appendix 2

Application of work levels theory to the youth service

DESCRIPTION	TYPICAL WORK	POSSIBLE ROLE

Level 1: Prescribed output

Dealing with immediate concrete tasks under instruction. No expectation of decisions on individual needs or variation of practice without reference or approval.	Running the centre coffee bar; collecting subs; completing membership forms; driving a minibus; supervising a sports activity; undertaking routine administrative tasks.	Volunteer, instructor, part-time worker, clerical assistant.

Level 2: Situational response

Dealing with situational needs, and varying practice and procedures accordingly. Work is concerned with appraising needs, and there is the expectation that changing needs can be responded to as they arise.	Running a youth centre; organising a programme of youth work; organising a programme of group-work; counselling a young person; managing and supporting staff; helping and supporting a number of voluntary youth groups.	Part-time worker, full-time worker.

Level 3: Systematic service provision

For effective level-2 work, a stable context and system must be created. This work is concerned with trends and sequences of events, focusing on individual situations in so far as they are examples of new sets of circumstances that need to be planned for. Involves managing staff resources to deal with existing demand within higher-level policy.	Running an area, district, or local authority youth service and managing plant, resources, and staff; organising an authority's training programme; designing and implementing a service's staff development policy.	Assistant youth officer, area youth officer, training officer, head of service, principal youth officer.

DESCRIPTION	TYPICAL WORK	POSSIBLE ROLE

Level 4: Comprehensive service provision

Work here moves away from an exclusive concern with current service delivery. It is also concerned with considering other ways of delivering services, and meeting new and, as yet, unclear demands for services.	Running an authority's youth service; deciding priorities and policy; restructuring the service where necessary; planning, costing, implementing, and evaluating development.	Principal youth officer, head of service.

Level 5: Comprehensive field coverage*

Developing whatever service or provision is needed to respond to a general field of social need.	Running a local authority education or leisure and recreation service.	Director of education, director of leisure services.

* It is unlikely in our view that level-5 services exist at the present time. Rather, in the local authority sector at least, they are part of more comprehensive level-5 departments. More broadly, the youth service is located in a constellation of agencies and institutions whose focus of intervention is young people in the broader field of 'youth need'.

Appendix 3
Different types of manager in the youth service

ROLE AND WORK

APPLICATIONS

Line manager

This work involves full responsibility for the output of managees. The line manager assigns duties and responsibilities, appraises the managee's work, and forwards the managee's staff development, and will be involved in selection of managees at interview, prescription of work, and initiating promotion, transfer, or dismissal.

Heads of service, area officers, and heads of units or centres. Some part-time workers in charge may also be line managers.

Supervisor

Takes charge of a managee for a given period of time, inducting, giving technical or practical advice, assigning tasks, checking performance, helping with immediate problems, and providing day-to-day support, in a context specified by the line manager. Supervisors are often senior colleagues.

Senior practitioners or area workers who are involved with new staff, probationary year staff, or with staff needing specific support or help at a particular time.

Co-ordinator

This work involves bringing together people who are working in a particular programme or project, convening work groups, issuing plans in order to reach objectives, and keeping informed of progress of managees.

Assistants or deputies, project leaders, senior practitioners, team leaders, and convenors of working groups.

Monitor

This work involves checking and keeping informed of the work of managees in a particular area, making managees aware of deficiency in work performance, and advising how this might be improved. Monitors work within a context specified by line managers and can be seen as assistants to line managers, to whom they report on monitoring activity. The monitor role is often combined with that of the co-ordinator.

Inspectors, auditors, advisers, and team leaders.

Appendix 4

Project working papers

Working Paper No. 1 Project Structure and Ground Rules, April 1985

Working Paper No. 2 Social Analysis, June 1985

MDP 3 Initial Progress Report, June 1985

MDP 5 Project Officer's Report, October 1985

MDP 6 Staffing Structures in Participant Authority Youth Services, October 1985

MDP 9 Project Officer's Report, January 1986

Working Paper No. 3 Research into the Nature of Service Delivery to Young People and other Defined Clients, March 1986

MDP 12 Accountability: some preliminary thoughts, September 1986

MDP 15 Project Officer's Report, September 1986

Report of a Workshop Day for Part-time Youth Work Staff in Surrey

MDP 18 Project Officer's Report, January 1987

Paul Benians, *Change in Local Authority Youth Services*, Uxbridge, BTCU, January 1987

In Search of Policy: the political context of youth service, April 1987

MDP 19 Project Officer's Report, May 1987

The Concept of Policy in the Youth Service, June 1987

MDP 21 Project Officer's Report, 1987

The Management of Change, *Youth in Society*, 1987

A Model for the Reorganisation of the Youth Service, February 1988

Gillian Stamp, *The Management of Change*, Uxbridge, BTCU, 1988

In the course of its work, the project also prepared a range of confidential reports to local project management groups.

Bibliography

Albemarle Report, *The Youth Service in England and Wales*, London, HMSO, 1960

Becker, H., Geer, B., Hughes, E., and Strauss, A., *Boys in White*, Chicago, University of Chicago Press, 1961

Benians, Paul, *Change in Local Authority Youth Services*, Uxbridge, Brunel Training Consultative Unit, 1987

Billis, D., *Welfare Bureaucracies*, London, Heinemann, 1984

Billis, D., Bromley, G., Hey, A., and Rowbottom, R., *Organising Social Services Departments*, London, Heinemann, 1980

Day, M. L., Bradford, S. J., and Eaton, L., *Embroidered in Gold: equal opportunities and the youth service*, forthcoming

Hammersley, M., and Atkinson, P., *Ethnography: principles in practice*, London, Tavistock, 1983

Handy, C., *Understanding Organisations*, 2nd edn, Harmondsworth, Penguin, 1982

INSTEP, *Guidelines to a Staff Development Policy*, Leicester, Council for Education and Training in Youth and Community Work, 1985

Jaques, Elliott, *A General Theory of Bureaucracy*, London, Heinemann, 1976

Jaques, Elliott, *Requisite Organisation: the CEO's guide to creative structure and leadership*, Arlington, Va., Cason Hall & Co., 1989

Jaques, E., and Brown, W., *Glacier Project Papers*, London, Heinemann Educational, 1965

Junker, B. H., *Fieldwork: an introduction to the social sciences*, Chicago, University of Chicago Press, 1960

Lewin, K., 'Frontiers in group dynamics', *Human Relations*, vol. 1 (1947), nos. 1 and 2

Morgan, G., *Images of Organisation*, Beverly Hills, Sage, 1987

Rowbottom, Ralph, *Social Analysis*, London, Heinemann, 1977

Stamp, G., *The Management of Change*, Uxbridge, Brunel Training Consultative Unit, 1987

Stamp, G., 'A note on social analysis', unpublished, 1987

Stamp, G., *Some Further Thoughts on the Management of Change*, Uxbridge, Brunel Training Consultative Unit, 1988

Stamp, G., 'Some observations on the career path of women', *Journal of Applied Behavioral Science*, vol. 22 (1986), no. 4, 385–396

Thomas, M. J., and Bennis, W. G., *Management of Change and Conflict*, Harmondsworth, Penguin, 1972

Thompson Report, *Experience and Participation: report of the Review Group on the Youth Service in England*, London, HMSO, 1982

Weber, M., *The Theory of Social and Economic Organisation*, New York, Free Press, 1964

Youth Service Development Council, *Youth and Community Work in the 70s*, London, HMSO, 1969